Rupert Loydell is Senior Lecturer in English with Creative Writing at University College Falmouth, and the editor of *Stride* and *With* magazines. He is the author of several collections of poetry, including *Boombox* and *The Fantasy Kid* for children, as well as many collaborative texts, most recently *A Music Box of Snakes*, co-authored with Peter Gillies. He recently edited *From Hepworth's Garden Out: poems about painters and St. Ives* and *Troubles Swapped for Something Fresh*, an anthology of manifestos and unmanifestos; *Smartarse* is forthcoming. He lives in a creekside village with his family and far too many CDs and books.

Also by Rupert M Loydell

Poetry
The Fantasy Kid (Salt Publishing, 2010)
Boombox (Shearsman Books, 2009)
Lost in the Slipstream (Original Plus, 2009)
An Experiment in Navigation (Shearsman Books, 2008)
Ex Catalogue (Shadow Train, 2006)
The Smallest Deaths (bluechrome, 2006)
A Conference of Voices (Shearsman Books, 2004)
Familiar Territory (bluechrome, 2004)
The Museum of Light (Arc Publications, 2003)
Home All Along (Chrysalis Poetry, 1999)

Collaborations
A Music Box of Snakes [with Peter Gillies]
　　　　　　(The Knives Forks and Spoons Press, 2010)
Serviceable Librettos for the Deaf [with Nathan Thompson]
　　　　　　(Champagne Troglodyte, 2010)
Memos to Self [with Nathan Thompson] (Underhand Behavior, 2009)
Overgrown Umbrellas [with Peter Dent] (Lost Property, 2008)
Risk Assessment [with Robert Sheppard] (Damaged Goods, 2006)
Make Poetry History [with Luke Kennard]
　　　　　　(Miraculous Breath Books, 2006)
Shaker Room [with Lee Harwood] (Transignum, 2005)
Snowshoes Across the Clouds [with Robert Garlitz] (Stride, 2004)
Eight Excursions [with David Kennedy]
　　　　　　(The Cherry On The Top Press, 2003)
The Temperature of Recall [with Sheila E. Murphy]
　　　　　　(Trombone Press, 2002)
A Hawk into Everywhere [with Roselle Angwin] (Stride, 2001)

Editor
Smartarse (The Knives Forks and Spoons Press, 2011)
From Hepworth's Garden Out (Shearsman Books, 2010)
Troubles Swapped for Something Fresh (Salt, 2009)
Voices for Kosovo (Stride, 1999)
My Kind Of Angel: i.m. William Burroughs
　　　　　　(A Stride Conversation Piece, 1998)

Wildlife

Rupert M Loydell

Shearsman Books

First published in the United Kingdom in 2011 by
Shearsman Books
58 Velwell Road
Exeter EX4 4LD

http://www.shearsman.com/

ISBN 978-1-84861-152-8

Acknowledgements
*The Delinquent, Envoi, The Frogmore Papers, Great Works,
Hanging Johnny, In Their Own Words* (Bank Street Arts, Sheffield),
*The Journal, Litter, The Matthews House Project,
A Music Box of Snakes* (The Knives Forks and Spoons Press),
nth Position, Overgrown Umbrellas (Lost Property),
Poetic Pilgrimages (Poetry Salzburg), *Pen Pusher, Stride, Whip*

Thanks
to Alice and her sister, who inadvertently caused much of this;
and to Peter, Peter, Alan, Meredith, Bob, Nathan and Nick.

Author's Note
No animals were harmed
in the making of these poems.

Contents

Wildlife

'The first principle of transformation is to move so gradually that nothing seems to happen until—without having created any resistance—it's already happened.'
  —John Haskell, *American Purgatorio*

'When there are no places left for us,
we'll still talk in order to make things true'
  —Anne Michaels, 'What the Light Teaches'

'Everyone was trying to be the best
animal they could be.'
  —Alex Lemon, 'Dourine'

Departure

In the beginning was the mirror
then the voodoo wagon arrived
along with experience
and a cryptic email mentioning death.
You said life was like a set of random marks:

spaces, paths and rivers, dance or song
disturbed the landscape,
forest and meadow provided the chaos
that leads to the suicide cliff.
I phoned to see if you were alright,

would like to be the mother of my children
and understand better the closeness
between the present and the past
but with jump cuts, fast forward and reverse
I must now confront my own reflection.

The future is down a little dirt road
in a rainstorm; watercolour is so exciting.
Field stones shaped like heads look
back at me as I arrest things in limbo,
fighting depression and defying gravity.

Animals Are Not Your Friends

You have to get to the point of thinking
with no flux whatsoever, only
thin polythene strips poetically animated
between air currents,
submerged memories and narratives.

Animals are not your friends. You have to go
to the point of thinking like this
then turn your attention to how letters
gather in an ever changing geometry
and begin to build their own nests.

The poem begins to weep. You had
to be there to get the point of thinking
like that. There is no decent way
to say this: it is our moral duty
to try to imagine what was lost.

Animals are not your friends. They lie.
The egret on the river bank turned out
to be a plastic bag trapped in the reeds
and the fox overturned all the bins.
My daughter peels a sticker from the page:

"Look, Daddy, we can stand up in the sky."

Wildlife

for Jessica

An egret and a fox, a small group of swans,
the tiddler you caught at the beach
and several small spiders are all that we have.

Bill brought along big sheets of paper,
asking if you could draw crows,
but you drew ants in a wood,

misremembering the shapes of trees
and how many legs insects have.
They are beautiful pictures, done

in your enthusiastic first encounter
with chalks and stick charcoal.
Flat out on the studio floor

you talk and tutor yourself
through a tall forest
of animals, dreams and ideas.

Animals Are Not Your Friends

I have got to the point of thinking
without being aware that I am.
I see with my eyes open and listen
with my eyes closed. Previous remarks
have got lost in the fog.

Animals are not your friends. The fox
killed the grass snake, chewed off its head
and left us the rest, which startled me
yesterday morning. Suddenly it's the final day,
almost time to go back to work.

I have got to the point of thinking that
I don't need to think like this. I cannot
formulate the rules or agree to sponsor
a friend. Don't ask me where I am going,
it depends which bus arrives first.

Animals are not your friends. The monster
lives behind the cupboard and something is
under the stairs. You can't pretend not
to have noticed. It's wild and wet out there
and all this writing is making me ill.

"You do know that this can't go on?"

Animals Are Not Your Friends

You have to get to the point of thinking
your way out of the maze. We have
already gone digital and gone on the blink,
all know that metaphor is just a roundabout
way to say the same thing.

Animals are not your friends. They won't
stand still and they have a fear of music,
a distrust of strangers and an inability
to answer back. Scenes come out of nowhere,
only one thing is sure.

If you cannot get the point of thinking like that
then at least make sure of the facts. X is a story
all about grapes and Y is a long winter journey.
I don't believe in synchronicity because it
always happens at the same time.

Animals are not your friends. One is not
supposed to be prepared or be afraid of goats
but it is pleasant feeling scared. And whilst
it might have been wiser to be accompanied
on a night like this it's not half as much fun.

"Whatever you do will be wrong."

Rescue Mission

Vital information flows freely from mind to page
but I see nothing but chaos and disorder,
ideas about the sanctity of private property
and moral panic about youth.

Knitting or buttoning a coat can induce agony,
where writing becomes a scrawl,
teacups rattle against saucers
and sleeping dragons awake.

Panic, though not without reason,
is fundamentally without cause.
This poem still retains traces;
I don't think I've stopped all week.

Write it in magic marker on your bottom:
smudged capitals, with the word (PANIC)
written smaller and in parentheses.
Now run naked through the shopping arcade.

Reborn, I am ready to be my own design.
This morally blank world is still
the home of my random babbling.
I'll take Zen over frantic meltdown any day.

Animals Are Not Your Friends

I'm almost at the point of thinking that
there is no reason to go on. We are
thousands and thousands of pounds in debt
with piles of books and nowhere to live,
neighbours full of urgent wisdom.

Animals are not your friends. Without
the sting it's just a stripe, without meaning
it's random thought. Structure and surprise
are not the same, people on the street
just complicate the shadows.

You get to the point of thinking no, not ever,
no, not ever again. Then move over to
make room for the rest of the poem.
All these moments of nostalgia
could be made to fill an afternoon.

Animals are not your friends. We will
wake up tomorrow to just the same,
remembering yesterday's sun. Vectors
and trajectories muddle in my mind
and I need to find a solution.

"Say what you've got to say and get out."

Ink Blots

There's a lovely sense of tumbledown-ness
when your question parts company with intent
and takes on a life of its own. I'm not sure

about the last line or your diction as a whole,
but the scatterbomb approach makes narrative
tricky to follow, as slippery to hold as the wind.

Whisper to me of far away memories, good reads,
new films and moments still to come. Let error be:
rumination doesn't need a ready-made finish,

roads don't need maps to find their own way.
I used to know the word for man-made paths
that cut across corners and common ground

trying to get there in a straight line. As the
crow flies is tricky, nature in extreme; you'll
never catch the ink-blot bird as he dodges

and dissects the sky. If I've misread anything
then please assume it was deliberate; poems
are often stronger without anywhere to go.

The Hard Sell
for & from Peter Dent

Narrative is made from melted moments,
broken glass from forgotten windows.
If you join today, confusion and striation
will be the mind's snowstorm. More cursing
and you will render time null and void,
without story or semblance of a future;
it will be difficult to set off down the road.

If you associate misconduct with discovery,
we will include a ready reckoner with
the chance to leap from a high place
of our choice. Your life may depend on it,
so tell us if you have a nomadic tendency
or ever go out looking for intensity.
Don't forget to let the reader imagine

and forget about total system failure.
Just stay in touch and try to remember
how great the boom in nostalgia was.
The last time grace erupted, it was
only a draft version, so make sure
you always have a drink in hand
and send us all your money now.

Reply

for & from Peter Dent

Yes, I know how distant you are
& why you check the starshine.
Your dream will never be perfect,
fenceposts never totally upright,
and the clouds won't stay on track.

There will always be questions
to which only I have the answers.
Don't dismiss me as kind; even when
the angel song sounds sweet
it does not mean I'm at home.

You can see me, true, but I
see you more clearly. Contrition
does not engender forgiveness,
and my mind helter-skelters
whenever you tell me your stories.

You can try to call in a favour
but don't expect me to listen.
Prayer is not the right excuse;
you must learn to recondition light
& make sure darkness never falls.

A dozen types of grey only emphasise
nostalgia; the poets' field hospital
is a state of mind, not a place to stay.
Abstraction wipes all detail from the plate,
religion is more thorny than you think.

Animals Are Not Your Friends

You have to get to the point of thinking about
enjoying each day as it comes.
All you can leave are trails in the desert
or stones in a cairn, abandoned dwellings
under the new lake caused by the dam.

Animals are not your friends. I want
to know more about life on the seashore,
sandhoppers and fishes, seagulls and flies.
The waders are wading, the children are eating
and the cat is outside, asleep in the leaves.

I've got to the point of thinking that
all I am doing is trying to find home.
I know what I am and it's not very pretty;
my stories are hidden deep down inside,
unfeeling and scarred like grey healed skin.

Animals are not your friends. You get
to the point of thinking only for yourself.
Books are as dumb as the dogs you despise,
handed-down skills and maps are much better
for exploring the meeting of distance and time.

"Ignorance does not inspire."

Animals Are Not Your Friends

I have got to the point of thinking that
one and one might sometimes really make two.
My daughter grasped the idea quicker than me,
was easily convinced. I prefer the enormous power
of doubt and reticence.

Animals are not your friends. It's next
door's cat that kills the birds, the goose
that honks and hisses as it blocks the way.
Everyone gets made redundant in the end,
why are you so surprised?

I have got to the point of thinking that
first appearances always count.
Beneath the breeze there are only dry leaves
and piles of grass cuttings from the lawn.
Breathe in and listen to the birds.

Animals are not your friends. Everyone
has trouble sleeping and you can count me in.
I'm up early like an overweight lark,
drinking in the light. Later I make coffee
and hide out in my room.

"There is nothing left besides regret."

Animals Are Not Your Friends

You have to get the point of not thinking,
I always find that that helps. I'm tired of words
and language, bored with village life,
the way specks of dust insist on always
drifting in the sun.

Animals are not your friends. They make
their mark and then move on, leaving a hollow
in the garden, a trail of scent you cannot smell.
The heat is on and golden July leads to chrome
September, just like it did last time.

You have to get the point of not thinking
about money all the time. Supplement
your income by selling tears or blood,
explore the simple strangeness of pale limbs,
driftwood laid out in a line.

Animals are not your friends. They bite
and howl, disturb the night, and shouting
does not help. This is speech we cannot ever
hope to comprehend; a dialogue with place
and nature, matters of instinct, not of mind.

"I am an extremely busy man."

Notes From the War Against Going Mad

It's strange, the pictures people make of me
that I don't recognise. For instance,
you thought me wearing a hoodie was bizarre.

Right now, I envy the dippy girl with the laptop
and a pot of muesli, who's drifting through life
without touching the sides, in contrast to my friction burns.

Time has a way of dragging me down and I'm impatient
for silence and order. The world does not oblige,
however many hanging baskets put outside the station,

newly painted to look smart. Our train accelerates
up the track, the children move in ever-widening circles
and you send medical reports in from the place

where things have a tendency to break down.
Every autumn it gets darker, summer gets derailed
and we both get confused. You're no happier than I am,

except for sunny afternoons spent sailing, picnics on the beach.
Take note: we are never going to catch up with ourselves
or be that young again. The airport is several stops

and a taxi ride away, the text says you've lost a schoolbag,
do I know where it is? I don't. I don't know nothing anymore,
am barely catching breath. There's a painting of a steam train

in a valley with a real steam train sat in front. These are notes
from the war against going mad, love letters from the unloved.
I will file them, re-read them, then kiss you all goodbye.

Animals Are Not Your Friends

I am beyond the point of thinking about
if it's blood or paint under my nails.
Once you have learnt to live on poison
and finish unfinished food you can start
to pay attention to the immanence of spring.

Animals are not your friends. The farthest
place away you can imagine is still too near
for me. In a room, in the rain, in the place
we began, are dreams of a summer
where the sun is shining still.

I am beyond the point of thinking about love.
It is such a clumsy word to sing
and always sounds so out of tune.
This small village has only a few places to walk
so tell me about myself.

Animals are not your friends. If you look
hard enough you will find a reason why.
At night dark holes stare up at the sky
and the lights in the houses go out—
an all too sudden departure.

"Nothing will ever grow."

A Box of Broken Things

The drawing is longer than the paper
and the paper doesn't stretch to where
the image waits to be. This gift from god
leaves us shortchanged, treading water,
with nowhere to keep our secrets.

The body is bigger than the box, we had to
break his legs and fold the arms to fit.
Death doesn't stretch to where we wanted
it to be, splintered faith is no use at all
if you are trying to hold on to belief.

The parts are bigger than the whole. Kicking
the corpse around, like ideas, gets us nowhere
fast. Germs of ideas, crumbs on the floor,
husks of meaning and every kiss I ever had . . .
Believe me, this is not the ideal time of life,

just the time of day when things go quiet,
the time when we bury ourselves and hope
to be rescued. The voices come only some
of the time but terror is always at the door
waiting. Revenge is best not served at all

as there is no time for silence and nothing
which can justify us keeping quiet. We cannot
lie or keep our anger in check. If we do
we will be silenced for ever: sniper fire
across no-man's land toward us, the page

full of holes, echoes of wounded voices
calling out. They will not give us even
the time of day, will not break the circle
of memory next to the open coffin
which still lies beside us on the floor.

The Guest Poet Answers
the Students' Questions

Have you seen the things I've seen?
The dying on the floor, the patients
mouthing nonsense to themselves,
abandoned children on the street.
Rough it up, stop riffing on your theme,
make sure you have something to say.
Coy surrealism is not the answer,

it doesn't change a thing, but I have
to write, try to make people read.
Is it a kind of healing? Yes, but
more of a sticking plaster than
a cure; the images come back.
I cannot undo the life I've lived,
wouldn't want to anyway. I am

attempting to be happy but upset
about how I fail. These things are
too awful to ignore, too serious
to be entertaining. They haunt
and frighten me, there are no apt
metaphors or sudden easy rhymes.
Why ask these questions anyway?

Why or Maybe Because

Call me naïve but I didn't know history
did that kind of thing to other people.
I am reading about smoke rising
from crematorium chimneys,
listening to glass breaking in the ghettos
although the same sounds spilled from cities
that chose to catch the bombs we dropped.
Some people say it didn't happen,
others polish the medals on their chest
and strut down the street toward the grave
it is difficult to find without a cemetery map.
No-one knows exactly how he died
or if perhaps he managed to escape.
He might live in the village,
be sanding down his boat right now,
in sunshine on the quay. Yes,
after yesterday's rain the sun came out,
ready for washing day. The tumble dryer
always works better if it's warm outside;
I can't be bothered with baskets and pegs,
it's easier to twist the switch then walk
away, collect it later in the day.
Anyway, it seems wars happen,
that battle lines get drawn. I've been out
in the studio, but only to take photos
of work that is finally dry. Cool knowledge
does not help us find the answers,
you must sift through husks and shells,
gathering up the facts. Call me impetuous,
but it doesn't seem to matter. It's the past,
and before the sun goes down everything
will change. Wouldn't it be funny if

we knew all the answers, didn't have to ask.
Do you remember any of the answers
to those questions we used to ask?
It might be best if you forgot them now;
why or maybe because.

Animals Are Not Your Friends

What is the point of thinking like that?
All you expose is yourself. As we realise
it's going to be another late night the pressure
begins to mount. Follow the adrenalin rush
then go and take the bus home.

Animals are not your friends. Look about
you and take note. We have learnt to obey
social courtesies and follow religious codes
but beyond all that is the sound of gunfire,
the unhealed wounds of truth.

What is the point of thinking like that?
It is the beginning of information overload,
a collision of headaches and beats. Hard to believe
we knew nothing at all about sampling back then
and still know nothing now.

Animals are not your friends. Look how
they hide away when you're near, all they want
is their food. There is a strangeness about them,
a dark and wilful energy even when they're tame.
I am quite a different beast.

"It's either me or the drums!"

Animals Are Not Your Friends

You have to get to the point of thinking
about the overall structure, how paraphrase
and referenced quotes direct you to the source.
Peter talked about the bigger picture
then painted one for show.

Animals are not your friends. It should
have happened long ago but it never did.
Now everyone knows about it and melodies arrive
each tide, beach themselves beneath the oaks.
There are bandits in these woods.

You have to get to the point of thinking
about something else, otherwise you'd burst.
I wrote to almost everyone I know
to see if they would make some art.
After ifs and buts and sighs they all declined.

Animals are not your friends. And neither are
my mates. Everyone has a season in hell
and this I take to be mine. I am wrapped
in dreams and still waiting for
colour to turn into light.

"This is as quiet as it ever gets."

When I Sleep

I don't know what to do with my arms.
They fall off the side or end up numb
under the pillow. Spiders build nests
in my armpits and my muscles won't
work in the morning. I don't know what
to do with my head. I drool and sweat
on the pillow, snore and grunt if I
don't get it right, drown in feathers
and dream of the dark. I don't know
what to do with my feet. Short as I am
they poke out the bottom or sides
of the bed, turn blue like the sky
outside. I don't know when to stop
reading or when to turn out the light.
Should I get up now or put down
my pen, turn over or rise like the lark?

When I sleep, I don't know what to do
with my bed. I'm not qualified for
dreaming, and can't follow those
do-it-yourself instruction sheets.
Should it be by the window or up
against the wall? Is a duvet or blanket
the best? I don't know whether to leave
the window open wide or seal the heat
in tight. Is breakfast in bed just common
or the sign of a cultured mind?
It's nobody's fault but mine but
I don't know when to do what anymore.
The light comes in at the window
each morning and disappears late
at night. Outside it is still raining as
I raise my arms up to the sky.

Animals Are Not Your Friends

You have to get to the point of thinking
outside of the box. There is a band rehearsing
in the lecture theatre that was the chapel
and used to be a shop, but how much more
exciting than song is a brand new poem!

Animals are not your friends. They dribble,
moan and howl, require too many walks.
I've rambled around a bit, but never as much
as this. Pathways and tracks are animal signs,
words are the sign of a voice.

You have to get to the point of thinking outside
while you roll in the dirt. Practice contortionist
gestures and abandon the trailer trash park;
take note of your erratic heartbeat,
use it to map out your life.

Animals are not your friends. If it still moves,
shoot it; if it tastes good, better still.
I am happiest hiding behind curtains or drapes,
think I am ready to dig my own grave.
But what kind of story is that?

"I wish he had written much more."

Not Sure

The cyber community is quiet today,
none of my friends are online. I climb
up the greasy pole to claim my prize
without radio assistance or back-up
of any kind. In the dead fish museum
the displays smell; if you dare to
press the buttons nothing happens.
Over in the museum of portraiture
eyes follow you around the room,
everyone is looking at each other.
I miss my igloo, am trying to map
the geography of anger, lose myself
in the corridors where these paintings
are hung. With my bicycle and bucket
I can fetch fresh water, with my stereo
and flag I can dance or stake a claim.
This is my mayhem: I have decided to
disturb the silence, leave tyre tracks
on the floor. I want to send an email
home, attach my laptop to the pigeon
provided. If this reaches you please
type in some kind of reply. I need help,
am travelling in circles between these
walls, am in the wrong museum. Send
something nutritious and warming,
also a hat and gloves. I left my bicycle
out in the rain, remember to feed the cat.
If anyone calls I am not at home,
if the doctor rings I am not all there.
Tippytoes past the children, don't let on
you know where I am. If I can I will write
to you later, more in the spirit of things.
Tonight, I will be back in my cage,
where the label still reads 'not sure'.

Coming Up for Air

The worst nurse in the world
has the worst patient in the world
in his care. He is impatient to be
in London, seeing art; for several
weeks now it has been pictures,
not words. He has just noticed
the initial in the author's name
is not the same writer whose
poems he has previously bought.

He wants to be sailing or canoeing,
to be fit and focussed, not killing
the hours in bursts of children's or
picture books. The water is up
to the overflow and the shower
drips. You would not like it here,
especially if you were unwell,
it is far too quiet to call it home.
He is sick and tired of being

tired. The music flows through
the wires and into his brain,
the studio is leaking. A month's
rain has fallen in a few hours,
each day is greyer than the last.
The heating has kicked in
and mist hides the high tide
on the creek. This has to be
the worst place you could live.

Places I Last Saw Him

This morning I'm on the train again,
leaving the village where madness has steam
and divorce papers have been served.

The car has died. I'm cursed by nostalgia
and fear, have spectacularly failed my MOT,
am close-up and off-balance every time,

upset at time passing me by, by the fact
I am dreaming with my socks on. Outside,
the kids run by, just living their lives,

although it is colder than I have ever been.
Inside, I am a little wizard of joy,
preparing to go back to work via the bookshop.

We don't visit because the cathedral's empty.
If we did then Cornwall would be nearer home.
Trains run by secret beaches I sang on as a child,

sandcastles rebuilt by strangers and their children.
Each day every summer I see him, and here's the station
where I cried, heading back up the line as the future arrived.

Indecision and uncertainty mock me. He would have
loved to have seen today glimpsed from the train.
Glimpsed from the train: a house we visited

hidden in trees across the estuary, in trees across the
estuary. Even this city where, this city where we once lived
and the hospice where he died. Mum has lived

where he died, where we grew up, for ever.
The park is still there, but now the alleyways are gated.
Everything knocks me off balance each time.

Cry for my dad and the fact he never arrives,
then back to work, to indecision and uncertainty.
This morning I'm on the train again, leaving.

Animals Are Not Your Friends

It's difficult to get to the point of thinking
like that, making art from just a few ghosts.
You think you've cleaned up then find paint
round the edge or splashes all over your shirt.
I can never uncomplicate life.

Animals are not your friends. You are free
to start reading wherever you want,
in motion or standing quite still.
Just pick yourself up and move right along,
set yourself down somewhere else.

It's almost impossible to get to the point
of thinking about death without breaking down.
You can rely on description or experience it
firsthand. Memory begins by rewinding
the pain; nostalgia is not an event.

Animals are not your friends. I lie,
they probably are. Fluffy and loyal, long-suffering,
they truly deserve to be called man's best friend
as they field requests and act playful,
intelligent and generally charming.

"We could but I feel like growling."

We'll Cross That Off Then

Slug rising late in the morning,
money melts from the bank account

as bloodthirsty characters from the resistance
apologise for what will follow.

They just want to repeat what they see,
puzzle at the performance of the world.

The reconstruction of historical events
is my favourite part of the book.

Voice control and unlimited editions
scale down the intervention;

one-sided interviews
are the least you can do.

Talk it up or take it down,
I am toppling off the page

in a convulsion of words.
Don't look down. I won't be long.

Foregrounding the Scratch

Begin by cutting out windows.

Overlay with the gradient set
then draw a rectangle below.

Fill the shape with a tone.

Colour where colour is
either a name or a value.

Draw a straight line.

Bring focus to the minimized;
note the three way turnout.

You have got a little lost:

background is actually foreground,
we as a people have it twisted,

will fill it with whatever.

Because of constant presence
this is often the best way to go.

Balloon Helicopter

I came away with the book on art
but no poetry or prose.

It wasn't like I remembered,
there used to be more of it,

and it was better made.
On the street corners buskers sang

and there were several bookshops,
blue sky over the cathedral.

The sunshine here is normally
filtered through the mist or rain

and it gets dark earlier than I am used to.
I have several escape routes planned

but the buses do not always run on time
and the blessings of xmas do not arrive.

I want to retire into warmth and light,
get regular pay with regular meals;

I think everything should be ordered.
Why is the moon out during the day?

Is it an example of imagination in practice
or global warming in action?

There is no stopping it now,
the scribbled line proceeds.

It is raining yesterday's clouds,
is not what I have described at all.

Learning to Write Lithuanian

A self-taught stranger works in darkness,
preoccupied with the alphabet.
A mix of abandoned materials
makes these sequences meaningful.

Cartographies bleed biographies,
mimic the source texts and files;
not just the process but the products
placed abruptly next to each other—

computer screens and headphones,
maps of works of art as well as poems.
No particular method guides this assignment;
image was the first thing decided upon.

We need more propositions for the future,
reconstructions of forgotten procedure
someplace else. I am not a sociologist,
just a result of statistical mapping.

Invisible trails people leave behind
them reveal the intensity of marks
repeated over the same surface:
landscape as a canvas for the imagination.

Let us pretend to be scholars.
(If only we had more learning!)
I am sat alone in the corner
translating my misunderstanding.

Animals Are Not Your Friends

It is time you got to thinking about
cultivating your own garden and spelling out
the beginning of a future. No tenderness
exists in nature, but the song's music
wraps them up in earth.

Animals are not your friends. What you see
you have not seen, it is totally invisible.
The amazing life of bees shows insect dancers
performing in elaborate costumes.
This is never less than entertaining.

Readers and writers are equally important;
it is time you got to thinking about that.
Stay on dry land and never put to sea,
try coming to terms with creativity.
In theatre words redeem acts.

Animals are not your friends.
There have never been so many household pets
or feelings of longing thrown into relief.
Whenever we write sentences
you must take them for a walk.

"You're no relation of mine."

Line by Line

This is the first line.
It comes at the beginning
and leads on to the next.
If this poem was more experimental
the next part would make less sense,
ask you to make an intuitive jump.
Motorcade treehouse hysteria school.
Did you see that one coming? Did you
negotiate the shift in mood or situation,
persuade yourself to do some work?
This poem is not concerned with truth
or experience, even being honest,
is just a collection of words on the page
a collision of event and meaning
happening in your mind. Soon,
I must go and cook lunch for the girls.
They want fried eggs on toast
but as the Barbies are covered in mud
their clothes must first be changed.
My CD of cello and mumbled singing
has been replaced by an all-girl band
and the sun is out for the first time in days.
My mother is still travelling home,
although we have not made the journey yet.
Earache has subsided but tiredness and flu
appear to have set in. If this poem wanted to
it would reveal more and try for tears
but as it is, my daughters are hungry
so this is the last line.

A Line Only I Can Follow

'The perfect journey is
no need to go.'
 —A.R. Ammons, 'The Perfect Journey Is'

Borrowing yesterday's make-believe,
I am mapping out the world
we sometimes choose to live in.
Here is the treehouse we bought
soon after we arrived. No-one
has ever really loved it although
there have been tea parties for teddies
and one summer you sat and wrote stories
at the small table we rescued from a skip.
And here is the shed I call my studio.
Look: unfinished paintings and postcards
pinned up on the wall. Under the tree
is my leaf pile. I burnt several years
of fallen twigs and branches just last week,
otherwise you could have seen my wood pile,
where a hedgehog hibernated for the winter.
I saw it once, when I took the compost out.
If a house is a machine to live in then why
won't the motor start? The perfect journey
does not exist: if you want to get to there
it would be better not to start from here,
but we came from somewhere else and
decided to stay, followed a line of water
around the city to see where the river goes.
They used to bathe elephants in the millpool
whenever the circus came to town;
beyond the houses are water meadows
that look like fields. We walked over
small bridges built to cross small streams

then made a kind of dam. An egret
fishes in a concrete drain, a pit bull terrier
rushes by, off lead. Under the viaduct
shadows divide the ground into frosted
and wet. There are tracks to and from
the river, others' makeshift paths.
A long mossed trunk is cradled
in the branches of another tree.
Today, this is my secret place,
the end of a line only I can follow, for
'at times, you must walk to the end of things.'

(The last line is from Patrick Ramsey's 'In Favour of Space')

Animals Are Not Your Friends

You have to get to the point of thinking aloud,
create a picture of the vortex of time.
The rejection of realism defines the avant-garde,
digital documentation rejects signification.
A white screen dominates the room.

Animals are not your friends. Leashed,
they articulate the plight of a certain kind of male,
bring word of good things to come.
The monster searches for answers, life
is bisected, everything is now.

Observe your own sperm under the microscope,
understand your thought is ill-defined.
All of this may be yet to come but will you
still set sail? Once again we need to find
a user-friendly route.

Animals are not your friends. Let loose,
they have a direct assault on the brain,
like children of the drone. Their humming
interferes with thought, provides a barrier
against both faith and doubt.

"We wouldn't want to sound too perfect."

Living a Life of Luxury

The generation of the beat
learnt to operate anologue synths
and turn their minds to music.
The pictures seemed to fit the sound:
sacks of rubbish were not collected,
the miners were out of work.
The students said I wasn't needed;
they might have been joking but
they ran a seminar on their own,
even set themselves extra work.
The clocks have gone back an hour
but I'm still tired and in the dark.
It doesn't matter if it is deconstruction,
reconstruction or just made out of Lego,
the assessment form has to be signed
and the essay submitted on time.
Rare is the record that takes the listener
to fields both verdant and desolate,
rarer still is a bus. One just went by
with DUPLICATE in its destination box.
Both of them declined to stop
although I didn't see the first.
There have always been doppelgängers
where I live, usually one of you,
who never leaves your island.
We haven't met very many times,
not at all in the last ten years,
but you continue to haunt and speak.
Do you still brew your own and live
mostly at night? Have you made friends
with the neighbours yet or ventured
into the pub? I haven't read

your poems recently but the books
are still up on my shelf with collages
and art saved from those days
when envelopes flew fast and thick.
Someone always looks like you
and surprises me. Once you were
a biker, once dressed as a sailor
in white bell bottoms. But I am tired
of saying this; every time we move
you are already here. There is frequently
a subversive quality in your work
and often a sense of loss
as you search for the magical place
through poetry, drink and song.
But I want to undercut my own seriousness
so please imagine this is something else:
a guidebook, manual or catalogue,
a roadsign or igloo. We must keep up
our momentum and forget to feel lost,
must remember to appear to be
completely self-assured. We are not
fooling anyone but they will never know
we know. Double whammy, double bluff.
Try to remember intelligence lies not
in the cutting but in the way we wear
our clothes. This is a style guide for the future
and you would do best to take note.
Partying allowed the government into power
and the invention of the drum machine
compromised the beat. Who's laughing now?
Who's dancing now? If you were in my class
I would not trust you with the scissors,
if you were indiscreet then everyone

would know. I almost said goodbye,
but all these things reminded me
and I felt compelled to write.
Simplify the landscape with darkness
and see if you want to reply. It is ages
since the days of teargas and plate glass
but things are never all they were
sometimes cracked up to be.

Music Out of Nothing

The shadow seemed to move, but didn't.
What was surprising was that that group
went away together and managed
to get along when here they hardly speak.
Adrift in a sea of footnotes and cross-references,
everything brings back memories of something else.
I wanted to speak my mind, wanted to scream,
but nodded instead, let it go. Yes, I would
like another drink; no, I am not on the wagon
although the steam has gone out of my engine.
I used to write and read, cycle, run and skateboard,
now I am more likely to succumb to television
and the books by my bed are from last year.
Can we be sure of anything? I'd like to think so
but the sacredness of questioning always intervenes.
How is it that now there is nothing more than words
the eternal is all around? If you peer through
the curtains you can see it outside. We are not
needed now but at least the rain has stopped.
Conspiracy theorists always blame somebody else,
it is easier and simpler that way. This is pop
and we can make music out of nothing.
It feels like we are at the end of a journey
but we've only just left home. 'Are we there yet?'
'No, sit still and be quiet.' Today has been long
and fraught. Look into the distance and try
to find the outline of promises and aspiration
as tables of green fields lead the eye away
into summer confusion. At the moment
wind and rain and tide conspire to flood the valley.
This is what the world was then but I am only human,
have run out of wonder, am dancing on the edge
of where I am probably not meant to be.

Animals Are Not Your Friends

What is the point of thinking like that?
You are and will remain on your own
if you talk too much. One use of solitude
is to re-interpet data and be certain
the right poem gets revised.

Animals are not your friends. This is
not about form or stream-of-consciousness.
Finance is a secret language;
vain and callous people are spending
all our surplus wealth.

What is the point of thinking like that?
What about fixed and static thought?
Museums and libraries burn to the ground,
leave phantom structures as the future starts;
contamination everywhere.

Animals are not your friends. They have
a relationship with shadows that lasts
only the length of a glance.
Coloured fragments show independent thought,
black represents our death.

"Private visions animate public campaigns."

Animals Are Not Your Friends

What is the point of thinking like that?
There's just enough heat to make fresh coffee.
Life's non-fiction so I read the last chapter first,
now have emotional baggage
to carry across the street.

Animals are not your friends.
They have no place in the passage of time
or the dictates of copyright.
Although I don't know your story
I am willing to surmise.

What is the point of thinking like that
with all these changes going on?
No matter how tired or sunburned you are,
foil reflects heat away from the ice
towards undeveloped space.

Animals are not your friends. Manmade
'scapes and gardens are less shocking
than the patterns history leaves.
Conscious choices made in the past
protect us during floods.

"Something is very wrong."

The Geometry of Summer

The angles in the shutter resist the angles of the sun,
capture the splinters of light which cut
the afternoon hours into lost minutes of silence.

We are resting after lunch. It is difficult
to pace the day like this, difficult to even think
of sleep after so few hours awake.

Sweat runs down my neck, across my mosquito bites.
Parallels are obvious but never meet. In the distance
the varied geometry of Tuscany I am trying to paint

when it is cool enough to open the shutters wide.
In the midday gloom it is not any cooler, I cannot see
to mix my colours; tones and shades all flatten out.

I painted a picture in the dark and guessed at greens and blues;
my daughter likes it best. My wife sees with a different eye,
her view all brown and purple: soft leaves, plump olives, shade,

with not a line or wall in sight and all the details blurred.
I am trying to capture light's scribble, water's flash and blink,
how the swifts arc above the pool through blue.

Animals Are Not Your Friends

What was I thinking, coming away alone?
There aren't enough bags on my back
to carry my books, and I'll never be able
to write or make anything here.
I am hard-pressed to even make out the words.

Animals are not your friends. The spider
is huge and the mouse is more like a rat.
The rat is a hedgehog living under the leaves,
the fox seems more like a horse
and the horse is the size of a house.

What was I thinking? I have lost
all sense of perspective along with
the will to live. Zany ping-pong guitar
and saxophone chaos make this world
noisy and beautifully warped.

Animals are not your friends. Their lifespan
is so short it feels like a lost cause.
Mercifully, vocals are often abandoned
allowing us to understand that music
is only a small part of the experience.

"I believe it to be pragmatic not banal."

Animals Are Not Your Friends

I am thinking that this can't go on
but I seem to be stuck in a groove.
Bars of light send electric colour
across the parquet floor but I can't even
make myself get on the train.

Animals are not your friends. They run
and hide, won't walk; fluff their feathers
and utter woofy words. On the way home
they cock their leg and spray the wall,
chase butterflies and dust.

I am thinking it might be preferable if
this didn't go on too long. Muddy marks
and snaking trails are my footprints
in the world. The field I have found
is starred only with daisies at night.

Animals are not your friends. They migrate
each winter and leave you in the lurch,
go on holiday each summer just when
you need to talk. If you take the longer route
you will be late for class.

"I need the element of chance."

The Believer

It's biographical, it's autobiographical.
All of it's true, it happened to me,
or I heard about it from a friend.
It's just the way life deals the cards.
Today I am marooned in the village,
the car's having its MOT at the garage,
my bike's abandoned in the shed;
I have never liked using the bus.

If this all seems terribly dark in tone
don't worry, there's light at the end
of the tunnel. You can get to the school
in ten minutes if you take the back roads
and drive fast. Ten minutes later you can
be back home again, ready to hang out
the washing or make your own breakfast
hours after the children woke us all up.

The autumn sun's surprised everyone,
especially me, who was getting ready
to roll up and roll over, ready to die.
If it rains any more we'll be swimming,
if it doesn't get lighter these poems
will really get dark. You won't know
what's hit you, whether to laugh or to cry,
phone an ambulance or read another poem.

One of the part-timers says they can't
do supervision, somebody else wants
the students to write global warming texts.
Nobody can fit any extra hours in,
there's no time for anyone to breathe.
I've forgotten about breakfast. There's coffee
and bacon, marmalade and toast, even
some cold custard from yesterday's lunch.

You must learn to make do, make your own
sandwiches, make it up as you go along.
It can't be as bad as everyone says.
This portrait of heat and light shows
your best side off well, the flames have
hardly left a mark on your barbecued mind.
I do not know what I am like, am just
an instrument of simple sensation and silent life,

always ready to make a diversion.
There are no reasons for knocking at
an empty house, there is no room
in the sanctuary. There have been so many
tiny deaths, one more memory gone
will not disturb the future or the past.
I have to say if you believe all this
you will believe anything at all.

Not Made to Last

The bus hasn't come again.
An old lady asks me for a lift,
convinced I am a taxi, doubting
that I am driving the other way
towards lectures and the weekend.
By the time I got to work
my poem was pasted to the door,
had become yesterday's news.

Words were not made to last:
all the things we say or do
might end up in this poem. Perhaps
I should write songs? This wallchart
shows all the bands that came out
of Birmingham, this the guilty secrets
that someone listens to. And this one
the world of jazz drawn very small indeed.

It is too early for screamo, although
I like the cover and agreed to swop
a CD for one of mine. I don't trust myself
twenty years ago, know I couldn't sing.
It never bothered me then, so why
does it today? Everything is slow,
including finding out the context,
which is now an essay anyway.

Symbols and cymbals glitter
in the mirrored distance.
These moments do not reflect,
do not compute; it's a good job
we have email or I'd never be able

to write to myself. Same day delivery
does not account for publication
date or the time it takes to get

from page to print. Two more artists
are not my friends, and Peter has
upset the poetry community
where he lives. Do not mention
Gary Snyder, poetry is tidier
than zen koans might suggest.
Writing in the gaps between moments
is a surefire thing, though snipers

are a risk. The black hawks hover,
unable to land without grief. Listen,
you can hear the echo of shots
and rush hour traffic on the road.
Structure is always a surprise; it was
never going to happen as you believed,
and belief was never going to happen
anyway. The strength of the turn

is where yesterday's crash occurred
and why it was difficult to get home.
We counted three ambulances
rushing by on the other side,
along the tide-flooded valley.
A teacher said we were lucky
to be your parents and we concurred
but now it is early next morning.

Your Longing Mind

It is the girls' first experience of death.
Both their Tamagotchis have died and
we will not be able to buy new batteries
until the weekend. Meanwhile, they will
have to make do without, perhaps help
me burn three years of twigs and fallen branches
in the garden without setting off the smoke alarm
or burning down the house. In the end,
I have decided to keep my half of the painting
black and white, the blue wasn't exactly right
and I couldn't ensure a consistently even texture.

I sent everyone the same poem, not one of mine,
because I thought it might amuse. This morning
a lawyer knocked at the door to deal with
issues of copyright and all my friends emailed
to say what a great poem I'd written, well done,
although a great poem was well overdue. Hoorah
for those who read the small print, acknowledgements
and the credits at the back. And shame on you
for only reading this far before jumping out
of the moving poem. Ejector seats are not fitted,
you will have to open your own parachute.

On Planet X there are all sorts of creatures
but little or no trace of rain. Crashing spaceships
into the ground serves little purpose
and only seems to annoy the little critters
who haven't yet been introduced. I'm not a gun
and neither are they, but you wouldn't blame them
for taking a pot shot, even if we organised
a tactical withdrawal. What kind of tactic

would that be anyway? The ghost has gone
and we have a bright view, windy blue
and misty round the edges. Winter keeps

threatening to arrive, but we haven't met
Autumn or Summer yet. Don't be a stranger,
come and warm us now, suck that smoke
in the garden away and give us retrospective
tans without the threat of cancer. If beer
without alcohol can be conducive to drinking
then think of the money we'd save
if you didn't bother to eat or to wash,
if you never bought any more books,
stayed away from charity shops.
This is the future and it's here to stay,

although over on the island, you have been
entertaining guests and workshopping
your dreams, in an attempt to make them
more useful when you wake up in the morning.
You need to obtain a temporary licence
and predict only what you need. Too many
close calls with nonsense leave you dissatisfied,
and you end up with half a poem on the page,
uneaten dinners by the bed. Pull yourself together
man and take the first plane out of there. And
please destroy these instructions after eating them.

Animals Are Not Your Friends

I am thinking about what you have made,
those drawings with water, circles of stone,
marks left on the hills or the beach;
about how you then let time and weather
blow them away into memory's book.

Animals are not your friends. They plunder
for their nest and forage for their food,
they run away and don't return, fight
other cats at night. It's no use limping home
to me, you'll get no sympathy.

I am thinking that it doesn't really matter
if you made those marks or took these walks,
or if you're who I think you are. There is
still mud on the wall and your photographs
where text and landscape blur.

Animals are not your friends and art critics
are all snakes. What do they know about life
or being alone for a week? A stone is a stone
is a stone is a stone. Look at where the path
might go, at the patterns in the sand.

"I prefer to leave things unsaid."

Trust Me

The audio visual equipment isn't working again;
this morning's lecture was short and off the point.
A man on nobody's staff list was using the room
for interviews, despite my prior booking. Work
is back to normal as though my cousin hadn't
just had a baby and it was still raining outside.
It is still raining outside and mist is moving in.

Carrie Etter is much better at drawing
in the crowds than me, but all the students
love Kingsley and are writing screenplays
for their final assignments. There is no-one
to supervise or mark them, as he now
teaches Film. No prizes for guessing
what the prizes are, just take the biscuit,

but not the chocolate one, that's mine.
Besides, it's bad for you and costs more
than you think. At this point in time
there is no point to make and no time
to work out who to ask. Online diaries
show Robert is just as grumpy as he seems
but oh so much better read. It is better

it seems to read than listen. Listen,
I am making a point. Do the research now
and make up the writing later. That is how
it is done. Trust me, I am your teacher
and I can teach you how. Do it twice
and email me your proposal. I do not care
about public transport issues or the death

of your pet; I am not thinking properly
and your pet will never work again. That is
the end of it. Give it distance and time
and you will feel the same. Our anguish
is not the same but the distance is or will be.
If we all exchanged ideas we could write
a group dissertation. The influence of Dylan

on Ginsberg and their role in the Beats. How
did Eliot get there? A backdrop of the city
shows Ez and T.S. aimlessly walking; you could
say they were flaneurs if you can find a quote.
No, Iain Sinclair is not a modernist, and Tolkien
was not his pupil. It is all fantasy, which is lucky
as I believe that is the subject of your proposal.

Now you must narrow down your subject
and read a little less. Make a mindmap from
your reading and build a book sculpture
on your desk. Take your work into new
territory, remember to exchange ideas.
There is no end to the day's events
and nothing on the lecture screen.

Learning Curve

Do not confuse slugs and bananas.
Salt will make them both inedible
and it is a cruel way to die. If you
step on a banana in bare feet
it will not be fit to eat. Chloe
cannot bear banana cake
or any sort of fruit dessert,
Jemma is stuffing her face
but would take pity on slugs
and snails, even when they creep
from under the rug that the landlady
has used to hide the hole in the floor.

Isn't this off topic? Yes, but it is Friday
and no-one wants to be here this early
or this afternoon. And no-one
is writing poetry either, although
that is the given task. What rhymes
with slug or banana? Why can't Jemma
walk past the record shop window
without cooing over the puppy?
And why won't she share her cake?
We are going to save slugs for her,
drink the beer that we would have
happily drowned the molluscs in.

Osmosis may be slow and painful
but that is how we learn.
Dylan Thomas is seeping under
our skin while slam poetry
keeps us awake. I have
a perfectionist attitude

and am good at inventing words,
am sorry I missed the lecture
but will probably do it again.
Criminologists say handwriting
can reveal a lot about the man.
Which is why I always type.

Asking Why

Some of the others were asking why
they didn't get into the last poem.
I said I couldn't force it, maybe
next time; perhaps they could be
more forthright and interesting.
But here they are, shoehorned
into the first verse, right before
whatever might come next.
It must follow a certain pattern
if the reader is to understand.

Josh Bell does it very well, but that
does him a disservice. His poems
sparkle and are the reason behind
these stuttered attempts to link
fragments of my life. At 20mph
parataxis causes a gentle bump,
at 40mph you get a serious crash.
Take the car back to the garage;
they will lend you a courtesy car
and mend it before tomorrow.

Bill wasn't in the mood to see me
although he proffered an interview
between Hoyland and Damien Hirst,
and was happy to eat my chips.
This morning we woke up an hour late
and had one of those panic starts
to the day, although everyone got
to where they needed to be and I
had breakfast when I returned home.
Nobody was in but I carried on

walking anyway. It's cold outside,
winter arrived yesterday afternoon
laden with boxes and gifts. 3 out of 5
children wanted to watch a DVD,
as long as it wasn't scary. It was,
so the eldest came into the kitchen
while the others screamed in the lounge,
looking away as and whenever required.
It is difficult to know what to read tomorrow
as it has been so long since last time.

I still haven't heard about the commission,
whose paintings they are going to use.
Pretty rude, really, after all these months,
but rather typical, too. The work goes on
regardless, series and sequences of paintings
no-one except me ever sees. A helicopter
disappears into the clouds overhead,
airlifting fairies from the garden
along with another year of my life.
My birthday girl is six today.

Last Day of Term

Stephen's new book has arrived with my quote
on the cover, also Charles' poem about death.
I will probably never see again the students
who collected their degrees yesterday. Some
have promised to write. Closure: smiles and
gowns, hats thrown in the air. Sound spills
from the stereo to rattle the wall. Yesterday
was the longest day in more ways than one.
How does it feel to have finished a year?
Numbing and cold, the rain hasn't let up
for weeks. The new grass needs mowing,
the shed is full of wood lice, the future
is a mirage. I can see what we are become,
can see we are becalmed. Bob is in Paris,
so much nearer than the States, but still
bad timing from my perspective. One of
the students is having a baby, its cries
will keep us awake. The principal, dean
and important guest of honour turn
their backs on us to address the crowd.
Haircuts and suits are in evidence, and
one green cocktail dress designed to
flatter the figure. Flip-flops are a no-no,
stilettos aren't great on these stairs.
We grimace for the camera, shake hands
with parents who don't know who we are.
School sports day is cancelled, the concert
went on for far too long. It is difficult
to remember what it was like at twenty-one,
if our paintings looked as derivative and naïve.
The free postcards are not a hit with the kids,
the neighbours have already gone away.

I have two hours before pre-school ends
and a million things to do. Thank you
for sending your poems but we regret
there is no common ground between us.
You didn't send a stamp so you will never
know. My youngest cannot differentiate
between wet weather and the cold,
is overdressed for June. I drain
the last of my coffee. There are now
several planning meetings planned
and the holiday has not yet begun.

Animals Are Not Your Friends

I know I should be thinking but I am busy
being mad, planning how to let my shoes
die abroad and have a holiday for ever,
wondering what I will wear on my feet
to make the journey home.

Animals are not your friends, even the tiniest
scorpions sting. Remember the one in Italy
that surprised us in the hall? And how
we couldn't work out what a leopardcamel was
because all the clues were red herrings?

I know I should be thinking harder but
my brain is starting to hurt. Last night
the fox that started all these poems was back,
except it wasn't him but a cub
intent on finding breakfast before dawn.

Animals are not your friends. Hedgehogs
scuttle away and hide, the penguins
just want fish. A leopardcamel is a giraffe
and, no, we don't want another cat.
You must learn to take walks on your own.

"Never work with animals or glitter."

Animals Are Not Your Friends

I know I shouldn't keep thinking about them
but why are there so many dead badgers
on the road? The speed limit should be
lower and the road angle is all wrong:
at the roundabout you can't see a thing.

Animals are not your friends.
They disappear when you go away
and make the neighbours worry,
turn up again the night before
you're due to arrive home.

I know it's not even September
but autumn is definitely here.
The grass is long but too wet to cut
and I'm due back at work tomorrow.
Autumn is definitely here.

Animals are not your friends.
They're collecting food for winter
and thinking about sleep.
Halfway between heaven and earth
you'll find this Cornish village.

"Summer flowers seed and scatter."

Tilt

People can decide for themselves.
Something is wrong and now is the time
to do something foolish.

I am recycling everything in sight
and I shall live for ever and ever and ever!
There is no planet, sun or star could hold me.

It is easy to write down what others should do;
you can't suppress information and
we sure could use some songs like these.

I'll be back in a little while
as there are other monuments to be built.
This is good but needs something at the end.

Animals Are Not Your Friends

There is no point in thinking about it.
It's not even September but I am
way past the point of disagreement,
almost past the point of no return.
Brainwash, it seems, is never far away.

Animals are not your friends.
No pets are allowed into the gallery,
they don't know how to behave. Besides,
wanting is more fun than having, even if
it doesn't help the art world survive.

There is no point in thinking about it.
Yesterday's painting by yesterday's child
is pinned to the wall above my desk.
Last week I witnessed the resurrection
of well-meaning rock and mass hallucination.

Animals are not your friends and it's probably
best that way. The appeal of steam trains
does not go away, neither do the memories
of your face on the giant screen. Lights shine
up into the sky as familiar music starts to play.

"You confuse listening with sensation."

Arrival

Some things you just can't understand;
the way the water runs uphill is one.
In this faux-modernist courtyard, yellow chairs
offset desert orange walls and tired succulents
I don't suppose are native to the island.

Walking all over, I found only the same;
have come back to yours to sit the afternoon out.
I am missing my own arboretum and
it's funny to be here after so many emails,
so long exploring everywhere else.

The beach is like every other beach
except for the circular walls. Couples
collect mussels and whelks as they walk
their dogs. Apparently, it's sunny at home,
not overcast like here, but I tell myself

I have a happy disposition and make
another mug of tea. Tomorrow will be
today in reverse, with a much lighter bag
if I can sell some books. I used to stand
there and ask why why why, because

anywhere seems a long way to come
just for the sake of a poem. I remain
convincingly normal, with no distinguishing marks,
and am cheerily waving goodbye to myself
as I wait for an ending to emerge.